Foreword

The case which Valerie Riches sets out here is overwhelmingly convincing. She traces the Gaderene-like descent of the last twenty years back to the more gentle slopes of the pre-war years, and then further back to early scientific and philosophical ideas which were to become so pervasive in modern times. Malthus and Darwin, to name the two seminal writers who are quoted in this book, can have had no idea where some of their unsubstantiated theories (for they were no more than that) would be leading the radicals a hundred and more years later. But it is nonetheless necessary to go back to early nineteenth-century thought if one is to understand the pretty pass in which we now are.

Valerie Riches' account is starkly factual. She is recording, not evaluating. Yet she speaks not as an academic who, all too often even in these hard days for academe, pontificates from an ivory tower without offering practical solutions to the problems he analyses. For she is also the driving force behind that remarkable organisation, Family and Youth Concern (formerly The Responsible Society) which saw the threat to the stability of society as early as 1970.

There are so many important lessons to be learnt from Valerie Riches' analysis that a Foreword can only hope to synthesise one or two of the highest significance. For the general public, it may come as a surprise to learn of the close inter-dependence of apparently independent and disparate bodies whose campaigns are, at first sight, eminently worthy. The "radical establishment", however, is not only small in numbers but is highly organised; and the paradox is that it can flourish only in the kind of free society which it seeks to destroy by the imposition of its own uniform values and practices. This inter-twining of membership is, in fact, characteristic of radical groups.

But to talk of examples tends to underestimate the commonalities between so many of the ostensibly innocuous do-goody organisations. Those who think that the movements in favour of abortion, of women's rights outside the home, of homosexuals, and of many other non-traditional spheres are simply a manifestation of our democratic and caring British society, need to study the evidence.

It is against that background that this book of Valerie Riches should be read. It is not the work of a bigot, or of a religious fanatic, or of a right-wing extremist. It is a summary of the evidence which a social worker who is a wife and mother has taken the trouble to collect about matters which have vitally affected her life. The rest of us can only admire the doggedness with which she has pursued her enquiries, often in the face of initial scepticism on the part of her friends and colleagues, and of indifference and hostility from many others.

So it is my hope that her work will open eyes to what is happening and that Family and Youth Concern will continue to attract more and more of those parents (especially) who may be bewildered by the constant attack on their rightful role. The time has come for a major counter-attack upon those who are destroying the foundations of our society.

Professor Sir Bryan Thwaites,
Former Principal, Westfield College, University of London

Winchester, January 1986

Introduction

As a parent and social worker, I joined Family and Youth Concern (The Responsible Society) in the early 1970's because I was impressed by its approach to the social problems brought about by the ravages of permissiveness. There was a need to analyze the social influences which gave rise to escalating figures of divorce, one-parent families, children in care of the local authorities, illegitimacy, abortion, venereal disease and the many other emotional and physical manifestations of human distress. It seemed more sensible to approach these social problems with the aim of prevention rather than coping with the effects.

Why, for example, despite all the sex education and availability of contraceptives, were illegitimate pregnancies and abortions rising? The more we investigated, the more we were astonished by what we discovered. In particular, I was amazed at the extent to which I myself had been indoctrinated with the current permissive assumptions.

The Society has no political or religious affiliations. It supports responsible family planning in its proper context for the spacing and timing of the arrival of children in marriage, as a personal decision for the couple to make in accordance with their cultural background and religious beliefs. In the same spirit the Society believes that parents, or loved and respected figures, are traditionally and fundamentally the appropriate people to impart information to their children about their developing sexuality. If sex education is given in schools, the Society urges that it should be treated with sensitivity by people of integrity, with the full co-operation of parents and with the aim of preparing young people for marriage and parenthood. The Society considers it essential that children should be protected from exposure to types of sex education which are amoral in content and whose purpose is to erode human values which have evolved over thousands of years.

It is not my intention in this paper to suggest that all those working in the organizations mentioned are involved for malign purposes. Many sincere people of goodwill who are involved may not realise what they are actually supporting. They, and indeed most of us, live according to a new conventional wisdom laid down by a relatively small number of radical men and women whose driving force is a mixture of new-found ideology, power and economics.

The assault on the family is not simply a national phenomenon, it is going on all over the globe. Until we can grasp the fact that the problems Britain faces are—or soon will be—the problems of the family worldwide, we will not understand what we are dealing with, or the size of the issues at stake, or how to find solutions.

The aim of this booklet is to reveal some of the driving intellectual forces in the concerted attempt to alter the future destiny of the family through the sex education of children.

The Network

In the late 1960's and early 1970's, there were intensive parliamentary campaigns taking place emanating from a number of organizations in the field of birth control (i.e., contraception, abortion, sterilization). From an analysis of their annual reports it became apparent that a comparatively small number of people were involved to a surprising degree in an array of pressure groups. This network was not only linked by personnel, but by funds, ideology and sometimes addresses: it was also backed by vested interests and supported by grants in some cases by government departments. At the heart of the network was the Family Planning Association (FPA) with its own collection of offshoots. What we unearthed was a power structure with enormous influence.

Deeper investigation revealed that the network in fact extended further afield, into eugenics, population control, birth control, sexual and family law reforms, sex and health education. Its tentacles reached out to publishing houses, medical, educational and research establishments, women's organizations and marriage guidance—anywhere where influence could be exerted. It appeared to have great influence over the media and over permanent officials in relevant government departments, out of all proportion to the numbers involved.

During our investigations, a speaker at a Sex Education Symposium in Liverpool outlined tactics for sex education, saying: "If we do not get into sex education, children will simply follow the mores of their parents." (1). The fact that sex education was to be the vehicle for peddlers of secular humanism soon became apparent.

However, at that time, the power of the network and the full implications of its activities were not fully understood. It was thought that the situation was confined to Britain. The international implications had not been grasped.

Soon after, a little book was published with the intriguing title *The Men Behind Hitler — A German Warning to the World* (2). Its thesis was that the eugenics movement, which had gained popularity early in the century, had gone underground following the holocaust in Nazi Germany, but was still active and functioning through organizations promoting abortion, euthanasia, sterilization, mental health, etc. The author urged the reader to look at his home country and neighbouring countries, for he would surely find that members and committees of these organizations would cross-check to a remarkable extent.

Other books and papers from independent sources later confirmed this situation. From Africa came *All Kinds of Family Planning* (3); from Colombia *The Structure of Genocide* (4); and from France *Un Complôt Contre La Vie* (5). The latter, a carefully documented book, discussed the geopolitics of abortion and population control as a means of exerting worldwide power by a handful of the "richest of the rich" who felt threatened by the rising power of the poor nations due to their sheer numbers and slow but steady economic progress.

A remarkable book was also published in America which documented the activities of the Sex Information and Education Council of the United States (SIECUS). It was entitled *The SIECUS Circle — A Humanist Revolution* (6). SIECUS was set up in 1964 and lost no time in engaging in a programme of social engineering by means of sex education in the schools. Its first executive director was Mary Calderone, who was also closely linked to Planned Parenthood, the American equivalent of the British FPA. According to *The SIECUS Circle*, Calderone supported sentiments and theories put forward by Rudolph Dreikus, a humanist, such as:

— merging or reversing the sexes or sex roles;
— liberating children from their families;
— abolishing the family as we know it (7).

Even though the authors of the books mentioned above had begun their investigations from different angles, the almost universal conclusion was that there is a carefully planned international attack upon the nature of the family and the value of human life.

The Ideology of Chisholm

There is no better example of the ideology lying behind the pressures for sex education than that contained in *Can People Learn to Learn?* by Dr. Brock Chisholm, humanist, and first director of the World Health Organization and subsequent President of the World Federation for Mental Health (8).

Chisholm was wedded to the idea of world government, and believed that those who opposed him were neurotic, selfish or mentally sick. He believed the most persistent barrier to developing a civilized way of life in the world was the concept of "right and wrong," a concept which he thought should be eradicated. Codes of belief, fixed rules or dogmatism, were anathema to him. Children had to be freed from national, religious and other cultural "prejudices" forced upon them by parents and religious authorities. He saw parents as dictators and suppressors of the child's better nature, and believed that sex education should be introduced in the fourth grade, eliminating "the ways of elders" by force if necessary (9). Chisholm's ideology is deeply embedded in the thinking of the sex education missionaries, as can be seen in many fashionable sex education publications and aids.

A Blueprint for the Sexual Revolution

For nearly two thousand years in the Western world, there has been a basic commitment to the ideal, if not always the practice, of associating sex with love and faithfulness in the context of monogamous marriage. However, towards the middle of this century great changes took place, quite different in nature from previous periods of permissive sexual behaviour. Among the most obvious contributing factors to this change were the *Kinsey Reports* published in 1948 and 1953 (10).

This work was financed by the Rockefeller Foundation. Alfred C. Kinsey, a biologist, applied to over 12,000 humans the techniques he had used in studying over two million gall wasps. From the data he collected, he proved to his satisfaction that there was no such thing as "normality" or "abnormality" in sexual behaviour, no "rights and wrongs." The validity of Kinsey's sampling techniques was challenged as soon as the first volume of the report appeared. The respondents were not a random sample of the population, but volunteers: it was only too evident that the results depended absolutely on the type of person who volunteered.

In spite of the inadequacies of the methods employed by Kinsey, the revelations in his reports quickly came to be treated as fact and were used by the media, "sexual minorities" and vested interests as an excuse for sexual freedom. Sex became a commodity to be exploited and love a subject to be avoided. It is impossible to underestimate the far-reaching influence these oft-quoted reports have had on sexual attitudes, sexual behaviour and sex education policies. The Kinsey reports provided the blueprint for the sex education missionaries—and the long term effects on Western societies are obvious.

The Fear of People

The population control movement had its origins in the *Essay on the Principle of Population*, written by the Rev. Thomas Malthus in 1798. In this he argued that the population would always increase at a faster rate than the food supply, and that the result would be an increase in poverty, misery and vice. The only solution he was able to propose was sexual abstinence for the poor. (11).

Charles Darwin came across Malthus' essay when he was writing *The Origin of the Species* and began to extend the scope of his work from the animal kingdom to include mankind. He believed that civilised societies weakened themselves by misplaced compassion:

> "With savages, the weak in mind or body are soon eliminated ... We civilised men, on the other hand ... build asylums for the imbecile, the maimed and the sick; we institute poor laws; and our medical men exert their utmost skill to save the life of everyone to the last moment ... Thus the weak members of civilised societies propagate their kind. No one who has ever attended to the breeding of domestic animals will doubt that this must be highly injurious to the race of man." (12)

Darwin's cousin Frances Galton was a psychologist who enthusiastically embraced Darwin's ideas and used them to formulate the "science" of eugenics. This is the belief that certain people are of a superior strain, and that the race can be improved by breeding selectively from them.

The question which immediately occupied the eugenecists was, how do you stop those of inferior strains from breeding and damaging the racial stock? This was the beginning of the birth control movement.

The two most influential campaigners for birth control, Marie Stopes in England and Margaret Sanger in America, were both racists and eugenecists whose primary interest in birth control lay not in assisting women to space their children, but in the prevention of births to groups in society considered by them to be undesirable. Marie Stopes wrote:

> "... society allows the diseased, the racially negligent, the thriftless, the careless, the feeble minded, the very lowest and worst members of the community, to produce innumerable tens of thousands of stunted, warped, inferior infants ... a large proportion of these are doomed from their very physical inheritance to be at best but partly self supporting, and thus to drain the resources of those classes above them who have a sense of responsibility. The better classes, freed from the cost of institutions, hospitals, prisons and so on, principally filled by the inferior racial stock, would be able to afford to enlarge their own families."

As an answer to this problem she advocated:

> "... The sterilisation of those totally unfit for parenthood made an immediate possibility, indeed made compulsory." (13)

Margaret Sanger, the foundress of Planned Parenthood Federation of America, coined the slogan "Birth Control, to create a race of Thoroughbreds" (14). Sharing Stopes' concern about the breeding habits of those she deemed "least fit to carry on the race", she drew up a Plan for Peace, which included recommendations:

— to apply a stern and rigid policy of sterilisation and segregation to that grade of population whose progeny is already tainted, or whose inheritance is such that objectionable traits may be transmitted to offspring

— to apportion farmlands and homesteads for these segregated persons where they would be taught to work under competent instructors for the period of their entire lives (15).

Neither Stopes nor Sanger had much chance of achieving their mass sterilisation programmes in the free societies in which they lived, and both detested democracy as a result. However the rise to power of the Nazi party, which in 1930 became the first political party to be elected on a platform of racial purity, finally gave the eugenecists the chance to put their theories into practice.

The Nazi programme to breed a master race moved swiftly from mass sterilisation programmes to euthanasia of the physically and mentally handicapped, to the concentration camps in which over six million men, women and children regarded as genetically inferior were sent to the gas chambers.

After the war, when the truth about these programmes emerged, the eugenics movement had to go underground and the term 'birth control', which had strong Nazi connotations was dropped in favour of family planning. Eugenecists and birth controllers had to find a new justification for their activities. The novel idea that the world was overpopulated gave them that justification. The population control movement was born.

In 1952 Margaret Sanger founded the International Planned Parenthood Federation, whose eight founding member associations included the British Family Planning Association and the Planned Parenthood Federation of America. The same year saw the foundation of the Population Council in New York by John D. Rockefeller III, who was also instrumental in persuading the United Nations to commit itself to population control.

Population Control via Sex Education

Both the Population Council and IPPF were and are extremely active devising and implementing a massive campaign for the acceptance of contraceptive technology.

The Pill was Margaret Sanger's brainchild. She established the Margaret Sanger Research Bureau which financed its development. It was the invention and marketing of the Pill in 1960 which put contraception on the map universally. Women were assured that now at last they had the freedom to control their fertility; sexuality could now be divorced completely from reproduction. They were told it was "safe" and 100 percent reliable.

It is not difficult to estimate the profits the Pill represents for the pharmaceutical industry. Nor is it difficult to imagine how important the advent of the Pill was to the sexual revolutionaries and the sex educators and their plans for a brave new world.

However, after a time of trial and reflection, it became known—though not necessarily to the consumers—that the new wonder drug was not so safe or reliable, but involved considerable health risks. But those who dare to publicise the problems associated with the Pill or its potential hazards when prescribed for adolescent girls are immediately branded as liars, scaremongers or in league with the Pope.

There is also a worldwide campaign to promote abortion and "temporary" or permanent sterilization, following the failure of the Third World to use contraception effectively. The campaign for population control entails a great deal else, as we shall see.

The fact is that IPPF's interests go far beyond the provision of family planning services to the underdeveloped countries.

In 1976, IPPF set out its *Strategy of Legal Reform — and How FPAs are Interpreting It* (16). It was clear from this that IPPF requires national family planning associations to find sources of law and arguments upon which to base reforms, reforms not confined to family planning services. Under the general heading of "the status of women," the reforms envisaged include women's rights to abortion, sterilization, tax reform, relaxed divorce and family laws, a lower age of consent for birth control services "to meet the needs of young people" and, of course, compulsory sex education.

To achieve its aims IPPF also encourages the formation of a climate of public opinion in which governments can be persuaded to accept responsibility for birth control services. And, as governments respond by funding programmes, IPPF affiliates provide a nucleus of staff around which the birth control services can be built. This staff trains personnel (including government staff), and in this way IPPF's activities are integrated with government programmes; maximum control by IPPF is assured (17).

This explains why we in Britain meet evasion and prevarication when we approach government officials about the activities of IPPF and the FPA.

IPPF's publications frequently emphasize the need to reach out to young people and implement approaches to population awareness, family life and sex education (18). The books and sex education aids recommended for the young by IPPF, however, have little to do with family life. Chisholm's ideology is more apparent: no "rights and wrongs," no barriers to sexual activity other than contraception. Paradoxically, this is an approach to sex which encourages in the young the very activity which one might imagine such education should discourage as inimical to population control.

To understand more fully the implications of the sex education the population controllers promote, the following chart prepared by Frederick Jaffé of Planned Parenthood/World Population is enlightening *(see overleaf)*. It was originally sent to Bernard Berelson, former president of the Population Council. Berelson obviously took these proposals seriously, for he included many of them, and even more radical ones, in a chilling speech entitled *Beyond Family Planning* at the Population Conference in Dacca in 1969 (19). Among his ideas some familiar themes occurred: inclusion of population materials in primary and secondary schools; direct manipulation of family structure; the promotion of two types of marriage, one childless and readily dissolved, the other licensed for children and designed to be stable.

A number of the proposals set out by Jaffé and Berelson have already been implemented in Britain, sometimes through the back door:

— compulsory population/sex education in schools (by the nature of Britain's educational system, the only subject from which parents have a legal right to withdraw their children is religious education. Once sex education is included in the curriculum, it becomes compulsory);

— sex education which emphasizes that homosexual activity is normal and natural, for teenagers, in spite of the fact that it remains illegal for males under the age of 21;

— tax system which penalizes married couples in favour of co-habitees;

— payments to doctors for providing family planning and sterilization services;

— the 1967 Abortion Act which allows de facto abortion-on-demand as a right of women (the consent of the husband or partner was subsequently ruled unnecessary);

— a free contraceptive service for all, irrespective of marital status and regardless of age;

— the right of under-aged children to contraception and abortion without parental consent (thereby making a mockery of the law of the age of consent);

— a series of "reforms" of the divorce law which now allow divorce after one year of marriage on grounds of "irreversible breakdown"

— changing the definition of the moment when human life starts from fertilization to implantation, thereby allowing the prescription of the morning-after pill.

Example of proposed measures to reduce U.S.

Universal impact   **Selective impact depending**

Social Constraints

Restructure family:
a) Postpone or avoid marriage
b) Alter image of ideal family

Compulsory education of children

Percentage increased homo-sexuality

Educate for family limitation

Healthy control agents in water supply

Encourage women to work

Economic Deterrents/Incentives

Modify tax policies:
a) Substantial marriage tax
b) Child tax
c) Tax married more than single
d) Remove parents' tax exemption
e) Additional taxes on parents with more than one or two children in school

Reduce/eliminate paid maternity leave or benefits

Reduce/eliminate children's or family allowances

Bonuses for delayed marriages and greater child-spacing

Pensions for women 45 with less than N children

Eliminate Welfare payments after first two children

Chronic Depression

The author of this char
Vice President of Planned P

Source: "Activities Relevant to th
the U.S." Memorandum f
Bernard Berelson, March

ertility by universality or selectivity of impact

on socio-economic status	Measures predicted on existing motivation to prevent unwanted pregnancy
Require women to work and provide few child care facilities	Payments to encourage sterilization
Limit/eliminate public financed medical care, scholarships, housing, loans and subsidies to families with more than N children	Payments to encourage contraception
	Payments to encourage abortion
Social Controls	Abortion and sterilization on demand
Compulsory abortion of out-of-wedlock pregnancies	Allow certain contraceptives to be distributed non-medically
Compulsory sterilization of all who have two children except for a few who would be allowed three	Improve contraceptive technology
Confine childbearing to only a limited number of adults	Make contraception truly available and accessible to all
Stock certificate-type permits for children	Improve maternal health care, with family planning as a core element
Housing Policies	
a) Discouragement of private home ownership b) Stop awarding public housing based on family size	

15

There is a great deal of propaganda through the media which encourages women to work, to postpone or avoid marriage, and to regard the ideal family as two children (or less) since children are costly and inhibiting.

There is also an on-going campaign to abolish or reduce the age of consent for homosexual and heterosexual activity, as well as suggestions that schoolgirl pregnancies should be aborted compulsorily.

Campaign Techniques

The campaign techniques which have been employed to bring about these reforms have been methodical and effective. They are recognizable in other countries where similar campaigns have taken place.

Having developed legal arguments, however specious upon which to base the reforms, IPPF affiliates set up groups with appealing titles to put pressure on their parliaments.

"Hard cases" are used to soften up public opinion. For example, "Fourteen-year-old girl dies giving birth in churchyard" is ideal headline material to sensationalise the cause. Slogans are used widely, like "Every Child a Wanted Child," "Safe Sex for Teenagers," to meet "the needs of young people" and "The Right to Confidentiality". They are used to prove that if that fourteen-year-old girl had been given FPA-type sex education, with access to contraceptives without fear of her parents knowing, she would not have ended up pregnant. Following such spurious propaganda we next hear of proposals, articles, research and studies to reinforce the arguments, none of which bear too much scrutiny for scientific validity.

With monotonous regularity, a range of women's magazines join in the campaign with surveys of their readers' opinions. These surveys are presented to the public as scientific fact, but of course the participants are volunteer readers of the magazines, not a random sample of the population.

There is publicity value in inflated statistics too. As Dr. Malcolm Potts, the international spokesman on population control, has said: "Those who want the (abortion) law to be liberalised will claim that hundreds or thousands of women die unnecessarily each year, when the actual number is far lower." (20)

Two examples will suffice. In France, figures were circulated to reinforce the arguments for an abortion law. It was said that 1.5 million or even 2.5 million clandestine abortions took place annually. The official French statistical organization I.N.E.D., however, prudently challenged these figures, and estimated in a report that the number of illegally induced abortions was 250,000. But even this figure was calculated on the basis of all deaths from obstetric origins for one year (1963), *as if all these deaths were due to abortion.* In another part of the French report, the researchers actually included male deaths between 15 and 49 years of age, hence doubling the number of illegal abortions which they calculated. So it appears that in France, men not only can become pregnant, they can die from abortions! (21)

In Portugal, the figure of 2,000 deaths from illegal abortions each year was spread about. But the *UN Demographic Year Book* for 1975 gave the figure of only 2,099 female deaths *from all causes* in the main childbearing years.

The Elimination of Parents

Of all the "reforms" achieved by the Family Planning Association and its network, the most insidious has surely been the removal of parental duties and responsibilities in regard to sex education and in regard to the provision of contraceptives to underaged children. It is no coincidence that Chisholm's "elimination of the ways of elders" has taken place in a number of countries. Indeed, there is pressure worldwide to minimize the requirement for "third-party consent." (22)

In Britain, by a process which I describe as the "inevitability of gradualism," the State took over from parents. It happened this way. In the 1960's, arguments were put forward by the FPA that making contraception available to the unmarried would reduce illegitimate pregnancies, an argument subsequently taken up by the abortion law reformers. On the contrary, rising figures of illegitimate pregnancies and abortions followed the easy availability of contraception and abortion. So the propaganda line became that a *free* contraceptive service would reduce the number of abortions. Pressure on Parliament culminated in the passing of the National Health (Reorganization) Act 1973. This made birth control services available to *all*, including children.

Following the passage of this Act, an advisory memorandum on family planning services was issued by the Department of Health (23). This included a section on the young with advice from the Medical Defence Union that the parents of a child *of whatever age* should not be contacted without the child's permission. This was at complete variance with medical practice in all other areas of treatment of under-aged children. For parents it was an impossible situation. They are held responsible for fines incurred by their children—yet they are not now allowed to be told when their daughters are subjects of unlawful acts. The Department of Health's *diktat* also had the effect of virtually nullifying the age of consent law without reference to Parliament, and it did so at a time when the paedophile movement was demanding its abolition, or its reduction to four years of age.

Despite repeated efforts to reverse the Department of Health's policy employing every democratic means possible, including Mrs. Victoria Gillick's private legal action seeking to have the memorandum declared illegal, the overwhelming will of the public on this issue has been ignored by the bureaucracy. Children have the ultimate right to refuse to allow doctors to consult their parents.

IPPF has made its position on this matter absolutely clear. In the report *The Human Right to Family Planning* it claims, under the heading "Rights of Young People," that the "adolescent age group (10-19 years)" should have full access to fertility regulation, information and services, with guaranteed privacy and confidentiality. (Within the terms of this report, "fertility regulation" means contraception, sterilization and abortion.)

Later in the report, IPPF asserts:

> "Family Planning Associations and other non-governmental organisations should not use the absence of law or the existence of an unfavourable law as an excuse for inaction; action outside the law, and even in violation of it, is part of the process of stimulating change." (24)

The proof of IPPF's willingness to bypass public opinion and contravene still-standing laws is contained in their report *A Strategy for Legal Change.* This describes how attempts by the FPA in Togo to introduce sex education courses in schools provoked considerable opposition from the public and parliamentarians. The FPA therefore undertook an active information campaign. As a result, the ministries of health and justice authorised sex education courses in the schools' curriculum *in contravention of an existing law forbidding sex education* (25).

No country which believes in democracy should ignore the power and influence of IPPF, working through national family planning associations, to instigate policies and laws which are damaging to parental authority and the structure of the family.

The Change Agents

In 1921 Dr. Marie Stopes founded a birth control clinic in London from which evolved the National Birth Control Council. In 1939 the Council changed its name to the Family Planning Association and became a veritable pillar of respectability in British society. However, profound changes were to take place.

In 1976, after the FPA had relinquished most of its clinics to Area Health Authorities, it concentrated its efforts on population control, sex education and providing information for the government on birth control services. Among its targets for the future were the provision of "suitable programmes for sex education in schools throughout the U.K." and "a volunteer youth movement throughout Britain which is able to put young people in touch with sound advice on sexual problems." (26)

The FPA's sex education activities are intrinsic to the central theme outlined earlier in this paper: a perfect example of Chisholmism. They sow confusion in the child's mind about the validity of the concept of "right and wrong" and present only one moral absolute: the use of contraceptives "every time you have sex." Lying darkly and deeply underneath the persuasive contraceptive propaganda fed to children is a sinister attitude towards birth. The misery of the "unwanted child" is stressed. For example, a leaflet issued by Population Concern, an offshoot of the FPA, carries the caption, "There's one born every quarter of a second." That, readers, means one baby. But the mental association of that caption with the expression about a fool being born every minute is unmistakable.

It is impossible to overestimate the power of the FPA in influencing thinking, teaching and policy-making at every level of British society. This is achieved directly through representation on committees of national organisations, and indirectly through the media, over which the FPA has considerable influence. The FPA also has its own offshoots through which its strategy for reforms can be achieved:

— The Brook Advisory Centres, set up in 1964, to provide contraceptives and (more recently) arrange abortions for the young. Its manifesto *Safe Sex For Teenagers* made clear its policy of providing contraception for girls under 16, the legal age of consent, and the philosophy that "the customer is always right." (27)

— Population Concern (originally named COUNTDOWN), set up in 1972 as a fund-raising body to channel funds to IPPF and the FPA to promote their sex education activities.

— Family Planning Sales, Ltd., set up in 1972. The profits of this contraceptive business, which rose from £10,000 in 1973 to £280,000 in 1984, are covenanted back to the FPA. The board of directors of this company includes executives of the FPA and the Brook Advisory Centres (28).

— Family Planning Information Service, set up in 1977, a government-sponsored and public-funded body situated in the FPA's headquarters in London and administered jointly by the FPA and the Health Education Council. FPIS has the power and wherewithal to spread the activities and ideology of the network of the interlocking and overlapping organisations—and it does so most effectively.

The FPA also provides courses for the training of teachers, youth leaders, social workers, doctors and others. Many of these courses are funded by the Department of Health. In 1974, the FPA issued a statement on sex education which said that one of FPA's goals was to create a society in which "archaic sex laws and irrational fears of sex and sex exploitation are nonexistent." (29) To this end, it should be noted that the FPA tacitly supported a report from the Sexual Law Reform Society which advocated, among other sexually liberating proposals, that the age of consent should be reduced to fourteen years of age, including consent to incest, the fear of which was regarded as "irrational" (30).

Throughout the 1970's, the FPA enthusiastically supported every radical book that came onto the market, including *The Little Red School Book*, later judged obscene by the Courts. Another book *Sex Education, The Erroneous Zone*, published by the National Secular Society, was promoted by the FPA. This advised that economic freedom would give girls the ability to choose as many lovers as they wished, of either sex. It also suggests oral and anal intercourse as methods of contraception, a suggestion which occurs more and more often in sex education publications for the young.

The FPA was also involved in the promotion of *Make It Happy*, by the Secretary of the Sexual Law Reform Society. This book seeks to undermine laws and social constraints which regulate sexual behaviour in any civilised society. Oral and anal intercourse, group sex, communal masturbation, incest between brothers and sisters, and sexual contact with animals short of actual coupling are put forward, with the suggestion that those who oppose such activities are old-fashioned and killjoy (31).

Taught Not Caught—Strategies for Sex Education was originally produced by an Australian feminist collective. The British edition was recommended by the Family Planning Association, and co-authored by a member of the FPA's Education Unit. One session described for teachers is entitled *What is appropriate behaviour?* The aim is "to increase tolerance towards a range of expressions of sexuality". Sixteen-year-olds are asked to discuss the following situations:

— Parents are in bed together having sexual intercourse when their three-year-old enters the room. They include the child in their embrace.
— A mother is changing her baby son's nappy. He shows by giggling that he enjoys having his penis touched. She continues to touch him all over, including his penis.
— A boy sits on his grandfather's knee. Grandfather strokes his hair.

Taught Not Caught was published at a time of great public concern over the rising incidence of the sexual abuse of children. The attitudes it encourages would do nothing to mitigate this problem (32).

Most of the sex education material made available to the young these days describes sexual intercourse in terms of "boy" and "girl" activity, rather than "husband" and "wife". It is difficult to find any mention of marriage as a positive and healthy relationship. Facts about the medically established link between early sexual intercourse or sex with multiple partners and cancer of the cervix are glossed over. So are the side effects of the Pill and abortion, whilst VD is presented as one more fact of life which can be easily treated provided medical attention is sought in the early stages. Homosexuality is included as another fact of life, as a normal and natural activity, in many sex education books and programmes.

The Health Education Council's booklet *Guide to a healthy sex life* tells young people "Sexual infections aren't always worse than many kinds of diseases that are passed around, such as 'flu or measles ... You need never catch an infection if you follow the advice given in this booklet." The 'advice' mentioned consists of talking openly about STDs, using condoms, washing the genital area after intercourse and trying to "keep the number of partners down to as few as possible". The avoidance of promiscuous relationships is not presented as an option (33).

Mindful of Mary Calderone's support for "merging or reversing the sexes or sex roles" and, in particular, "abolishing the family as we know it," it is interesting to note what the FPA has to say on marriage in its sex manual for 13- to 16-year-olds *Learning to Live with Sex*. The FPA explains that while marriage as a formal commitment by two people to live together may be an ideal for individuals or society,

> "many marriages do not work out quite like that. More people are choosing to live together without formalising their vows because they may wish to separate later on, and some people are more tolerant of unfaithfulness or other close or sexual relationships outside of marriage ..."

In 1977, the FPA and the Campaign for Homosexual Equality, with other "sexual minority" groups, organized a conference on "Sex Education—Where Do We Go From Here?" The aim was to include material about "sexual minority" behaviour as a compulsory part of the school curriculum (35).

The FPA's influence has been such that it is customary practice in Britain to demonstrate contraceptives to children in the classroom, often with the message that they can be obtained from clinics where no one will inform parents. Classroom quizzes and exam questions on contraceptives have also become part of the indoctrination process. As a spokesman stated on behalf of the FPA's Education Service in 1969, "Contraceptive education has to be given very young, it is almost too late when the children get to puberty ... children in school are a captive audience." (36) It was hardly surprising, therefore, to read in the Monopolies Commission Report on Contraceptive Sheaths that London Rubber Industries submitted that the FPA's educational activities "widen the market for contraceptives." (37)

The FPA's attitude to parents is entirely consistent with Chisholm's view that they are suppressors of their children's better nature. "Parents—they're the most dangerous people of all," said an FPA spokeswoman (38). The FPA advised the Department of Health on the memorandum on family planning services published in 1974, which removed parental responsibilities for their under-aged children. But even before that, the FPA advised adolescents to go to advisory clinics which would "treat your problems sympathetically and not tell your parents unless you want them to know." (39) The FPA and its offshoots bring all their power to bear upon parental moves to have their rights restored. The reason is clear. Lady Brook, founder and President of the Brook Advisory Centres, wrote in reply to criticism of the sex education missionaries:

> "It is now the privilege of the Parental State to take major decisions—objective, unemotional, the State weighs up what is best for the child ..." (40)

The End Justifies the Means

The British public is repeatedly told that nationwide sex education and the provision of contraceptives to teenagers are justified by the need to bring down the number of unwanted pregnancies. The whole exercise has been a colossal failure. Illegitimate maternities and abortions in teenagers continue to rise. STDs are spreading rapidly and acquiring new and more virulent forms like herpes and AIDS. Cancer of the cervix is now reaching epidemic proportions in young women, amongst whom it was until recently almost unknown. Its occurrence in this age range is often related to early intercourse with multiple partners. Yet the same policies are pursued relentlessly: more sex education, more explicit, and at younger ages; more contraceptives supplied at more sex clinics, to be followed by more abortions.

The ubiquitous Dr. Malcolm Potts admitted years ago this would be the case: "As people turn to contraception, there will be a rise, not a fall, in the abortion rate ..." (41) And again, "No society has controlled its fertility ... without recourse to a significant number of abortions. In fact abortion is often the *starting* place in the control of fertility." (42)

The reason has become obvious over the years: contraception and abortion are inextricably bound together. One physician and researcher for the Brook Advisory Centres has confirmed this: "Twenty years ago women were more resigned to unwanted pregnancy, but as they have become more conscious of preventing conception, so they have come to request terminations when contraception fails. There is overwhelming evidence that, contrary to what you might expect, *the availability of contraception leads to an increase in the abortion rate.*" (43) (emphasis added).

Research from the United States substantiates the fact that the more contraceptive programmes are aimed at the young, the more pregnancies, abortions, promiscuity, VD and cancer of the cervix result. There may be complicated contributory reasons why this is so, but the basic explanation is simple: the total of sexually active youngsters grows, and at younger ages (44), and the failure rate of contraceptives is high among teenagers, four to five times higher than among adults (45).

The reason why youngsters and the public at large are not told the truth is clear. Even though research (carried out by people sympathetic to the birth control lobby) has found that sexual experience in youngsters lessens the importance of parental influence (46), the same policies are pursued because *nothing* must thwart the ideology of liberating children from their families. The end justifies the means.

And What of the Future?

In this paper I have sought to expose some of the hidden connivances, implications, and activities of an interlocking power structure of which sex education is one—but by no means the only—concern. It is a lobby which has been described as "one of the most savagely damaging lobbies a society has ever had to confront." (47) It is damaging because the sex education it seeks to promote (under whatever guise it may appear) is a vehicle to spread an amoralism that is destructive of the family and of society.

When a nation is threatened by enemies from outside or confronted with economic policies which may damage future national stability, there is public controversy, advocacy of solutions and the emergence of alternative strategies and policies. Where matters of family policy and social morals are concerned, however, political and public debate seems to become stricken with paralysis, closed to scrutiny, fearful of the word "morality". Yet the issue at stake concerns the very fabric of society, the very future of the human race. The threat posed should command immediate response, energetic debate and the formation of counter-policies.

It is imperative that people of good will investigate and unravel the strands which have been cleverly woven round the policies, laws and institutions in their own countries. The instigators need to be identified and exposed, because they function with impunity, in secrecy or behind a screen of pseudo-respectability given when governments fund their activities and policies.

It is an awesome situation to contemplate and act upon. It is one which requires coordinated effort by those who believe in and support the family and the sanctity of life. It is a battle to be fought *now* by those who cherish the true meaning of freedom.

References

1) K H Kavanagh, *Sex Education, Its Uses and Abuses*, Family and Youth Concern, 1975.

2) Bernard Schreiber, *The Men Behind Hitler*, La Haye—Mureaux, France.

3) Michael Golden, *All Kinds of Family Planning*, African Universities Press, 1981.

4) Varlos Corsi Otalora and Marfa Cristina de Corsi, *The Structure of Genocide*, Bogota, Colombia, 1981.

5) Emerentienne de Lagrange, Marguerita-Marie de Lagrange and Rene Bel, *Un Complot Contre La Vie*, Societe de Production Litteraire, 1979.

6) Claire Chambers, *The SIECUS Circle, A Humanist Revolution*, Western Islands, 1977.

7) *ibid* p.14

8) Brock Chisholm, *Can People Learn to Learn?* Geo Allen and Unwin, 1952.

9) Brock Chisholm, *The Psychiatry of Enduring Peace and Social Progress*, Psychiatry Vol 9, 1946.

10) A C Kinsey, *Sexual Behaviour in the Human Male*, 1948, *Sexual Behaviour in the Human Female*, 1953, Saunders, Pa. 1953.

11) Thomas R Malthus, *An essay on the principle of population*, London, 1798.

12) Charles Darwin, *The Descent of Man*, London, 1871.

13) Marie Stopes, *Radiant Motherhood*, London, 1920.

14) Margaret Sanger, *Birth Control Review*, December 1921.

15) Margaret Sanger, *Plan for Peace*, Birth Control Review, April 1932.

16) *Strategy for Legal Reform and How FPAs are interpreting it*, IPPF News, July/August 1976.

17) *Her Future in the Balance* (pamphlet) IPPF, 1971.

18) *Selected Resource Materials: Approaches to Population Awareness, Family Life and Sex Education for Young People*, IPPF, March 1978.

19) Bernard Berelson, *Beyond Family Planning*, Population Control Conference Paper, Dacca, 1969.

20) Malcolm Potts, *Abortion*, Cambridge University Press, 1977.

21) Emerentienne de Lagrange et al. *op.cit.*

22) *The Use of Para-Medicals for Primary Health Care in the Commonwealth*, Commonwealth Secretariat, 1979.

23) *Family Planning Services, Memorandum of Guidance*, Department of Health and Social Security, May 1974.

24) *The Human Right to Family Planning*, IPPF, London, 1984. (cf. also *The Voluntary Sector in Population and Development* IPPF London, 1979.)

25) *A Strategy for Legal Change*, IPPF London, 1981.